LOVE & THE EGO

LOVE & THE EGO

A Lesson from Archangel Gabriel

by
Reverend Penny Donovan

Sacred Garden Fellowship, Inc.
Albany, New York

Published by Sacred Garden Fellowship, Inc.
Albany, NY
www.sacredgardenfellowship.org

ISBN-13: 978-1932746129

First published in audio and print by Appleseeds Publishing. Copyright © 1999 by Rev. Penny Donovan.

Acknowledgements

This book would not have been possible without the support and efforts of many in the Sacred Garden Fellowship (SGF) community who have helped to sustain and promote SGF's mission over the years. We also offer deep loving gratitude to the nonphysical teachers, guides, and angels accompanying us every step of the way, challenging us, offering opportunities for both the organization and the community to grow spiritually, and guiding us ever forward on the path of Truth. And finally, many thanks to the reader who has been drawn to these lessons, advancing themselves in unity towards awakening the divinity within.

Introduction

An extraordinarily rare and pure trance channel, Reverend Penny Donovan is a psychic and natural medium who has been channeling the wisdom of Master Teachers for over thirty years. In 1987, during her time as pastor of Trinity Temple of the Holy Spirit Church in Albany, NY, she began channeling lessons from Archangel Gabriel, who continued to speak through her until 1999. In brief evening sessions as well as day-long and full weekend retreats, Gabriel blessed us with over 250 lectures on a wide variety of topics relating to spirituality. His central theme continues to encourage us all to live our truth through love, compassion, and forgiveness. Since 1999 when Gabriel left, many other Master Teachers have come through Rev. Penny, bringing a higher context to previous lessons and providing more advanced and insightful spiritual truths.

Although Gabriel had given lectures on both love and the ego before, he brings them together in this lesson held during the evening of August 6, 1999.

As Gabriel has requested, care was and is being taken to transcribe his teachings word for word from the original cassette recordings, so this volume contains his words as spoken, including any interruptions, pauses, participant questions, etc.

Rev. Penny's love of God, her teaching and channeling talents, her ability to incorporate lessons in truth gained and developed from a lifetime of spiritual learning and growth, and her desire to help others find their spiritual path and highest good are a gift to us and our world. Through Sacred Garden Fellowship (SGF), a nonprofit organization she co-founded with spiritual teacher, healer, and psycho-spiritual therapist Donald Gilbert, Rev. Penny continues to share spiritual lessons at SGF's workshops and retreats.

Please enjoy this spiritual teaching from Archangel Gabriel as it helps guide you to live your truth.

May you be blessed on your journey.

LOVE & THE EGO

A Lesson from Archangel Gabriel

Love & the Ego
August 6, 1999

Archangel Gabriel:

It is good to see your lights, your shining faces.

Tonight, I want to talk to you tonight about the love and about the ego and how you can discern between what the ego tells you is love and what is really, truly love, because no one knows true love. Everyone has a misperception of it, so tonight we desire greatly to bring to you the truth concerning love.

Love is a universal force. You experience it through your egos as a personal emotion. You fancy yourselves to be in love or out of love, as the case may be, but the truth is that true, real love is that which goes beyond the boundaries of form. It is not governed by appearance. Love is. It is you. God created you in love. God created you love. Indeed, if it were to be told, *all* of life, any expression of life, is pure love.

Now, the ego has *its* version of love, and the ego's version of love is very different from the real thing. The ego indeed would have you believe that when you are in love, you know it because you are joyously happy in the presence of the object of your love.

When you have fallen in love with another, you want to be with them, you want to do things for them, you want them to do things for you. There has to be this togetherness all of the time, and you perceive that that be true love. And if you are not together or one says or does something the other doesn't like, there are hurt feelings, there's an emotional disruption there, and one considers that love has been withdrawn, or that perhaps that you can withdraw love.

Now, all of that is the ego's idea of what love is, because it is absolutely, completely impossible for you to have love withdrawn from you or for you to withdraw love from another. And the reason this be true is because you were created in *perfect, pure love*. It's the innate part of your very beingness, and because it is so, it is not possible for the real love to ever leave you.

Now, you perceive that you can withhold love or that love is a possession or is to be possessed. And love cannot be possessed, for love is free-flowing. It is the complete, pure expression of life. So therefore, for you to feel that someone can withhold love from you, or you them, is a great error. "Ah," but you say, "I have been in love and someone loved me and then they scorned me for another. Now you can't tell me that that's not withholding love." No, it isn't. I shall tell you what it is. It is the game that the ego...one ego plays with the other ego.

Have you ever watched half-grown puppies play with one another? There is always one who wants to dominate and one...they have these play fights going on. Well, the ego is very much like a half-grown, mongrel pup that wants to dominate, and anything that comes into its world it has to dominate.

Now, the ego, of itself, has no dominion. The only power that it has is what you give it, when you *believe* in it—when you say, "Oh, I can't do this because I am not well," or "I can't do that because I am limited in some way," or "My true love has gone astray," or something of that sort. That is the ego's voice, and that's what you are listening to and *believing in.*

So what is happening...you are not coming up out of the ego and into the pureness of your Spirit. You are experiencing the game of have and have not that the ego has created and has labeled "love."

Know you not how when you were young, it is very easy for you to fall in love? How many times in your growing up years have you been in love forever and it lasted a week or two? (Laughter) And in your teenage years, were you not helplessly in love with some entertainer or another to whom you would have absolutely given *anything* they wanted if they just would have bestowed upon you one moment's affection?

Now, that's not love. That is the ego's illusion, because the ego would have you be in love with that which you cannot have, because that is how the ego convinces you that love is not true, that love is a very *dangerous* thing and you must really be very careful of it. And it is the ego's way of keeping you off balance.

Have you not noticed that when you are in love that the world is wondrous indeed? Everything, including your job, seems great. You love where you live, you love where you work, you love your neighbor, you love strangers, you love little kittens, you just love, love, love, love, love, love.

But when you are out of love, nothing in your world is right, is it? Your job is terrible, you house isn't right, your friends have all left you. "Woe is me. I shall never be the same." And do you not believe that you shall never know happiness again? Now, that should give you a clue.

That should clue you in that ego is afoot and that it has absolutely convinced you that *it* is right and love is very wrong.

It also has you thoroughly convinced that you can live lovelessly. How many of you in this room at this moment feel that you would like to have love in your life but it is absent? Aha. Been listening to the ego, eh? Indeed.

Now, love—real love—is a universal force. It is nowhere absent. It is impossible to not know it. It is impossible to not *be* loved, and it is equally impossible to not be loving. "Oh," but you say, "I know lots of times in my life when I have not been loved and when I certainly have not been loving, and how can you sit there and say that?"

Because in truth, you cannot be outside of love, because that is what you're made of. That is the substance of the Spirit of you, which God has breathed forth and placed in you that you are made up of. That's all...the only thing that you are made up of is love.

"Well, then if that be true, then how come so-and-so doesn't love me anymore, or I don't love so-and-so anymore? How come that is?"

I shall tell you. Most mortals upon the earth fall in love first by looking at someone. Now, you are first attracted to another by their appearance, are you not? Their appearance is pleasing to you, so therefore you think, "Oh, I would like to get to know that person. I like them."

Now, the other mistake that mortals make is they expect the object of their affections to completely, absolutely fulfill every need that they have, and when they discover the other person can't do that or doesn't want to do that, then is when love goes awry.

Now, the reason that you think that you can find love in someone else is because you don't want to find it in yourself. Now, to love one's self, one has to be aware of the internal workings of the Spirit of you, and you have to recognize that this body that you wear, this personality that you have created, is not the real you.

Let us say that this little droplet over here is the real you. It is filled with the glory of God. It shines and sparkles. It is creative. It is eternal. It has absolutely nothing wrong with it. It is perfect, absolutely perfect, in every way.

Spirit

Now, while you are in the spirit, you know this. When you are in the spirit and you see one another, you don't see a form that you look at; you see this beauteous light, this glorious love-emanating creation that reflects the power and the glory of God. That's what you see.

Now you decide to come into the earth plane, so you create a personality. Well, the personality has no particular form. You sort of create it as you go along with it. You decide you want to come to the earth and you want to accomplish a certain thing, and you decide what kind of personality you would require in order to do that, and you sow the seeds of what you think that personality should be.

So, you place in this personality a little of the glory of God and a little seed in here. Now, you usually develop the personality in a very basic form before you enter into the physical body. It is never fully

Seed of spirituality

Personality

developed. It is very much like a little embryo, just as an embryo has all of what is required in the cells and DNA and all of that to produce a certain type of body, a certain color hair, a certain color eyes, certain bone structure, and so forth. This little piece of spirit life in the personality has the same potential.

Now, that is going to require some help, so it creates a mental body, which fills quickly with habits—thought habits—from the soul of you. Now remember, you have a lot of memory in your soul. It is the most complete, never-failing, always-right-on computer that you have ever imagined.

Mental Body

Now, in this mental body comes the ideas from the soul from past experience. Now, the mental body needs an emotional body. What does that look like?

Participant: Chaos.

Gabriel: Exactly. Your emotional body is chaotic. It creates chaotic situations and it presents them to you as a truth. Now, where do you fall in love? In your emotional body. You don't fall in love in your mental body; your mental body is not capable of emotion. So in

Emotional Body

your mind...your mind is still pulling on experiences from the past. It still draws on the soul memory and from it, it creates ideas and concepts, which are fed into the emotional body and the emotional body immediately decides, "This is tragic. This is awful. This is terrible. Oh, what are we ever going to do? The sky is falling. Oh dear, oh dear, oh dear."

Now, while you are using this emotional chaos, all of that is getting poured into the physical body. Here you've this little, old physical body over here that you are going to be living your life in, and what has it got? Way back here, it's got a little seed of the spirituality back in this still-forming personality. Would you write "Personality" up here? And "Mental Body" here and "Emotional Body" there. Thank you.

Physical Body

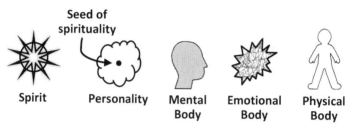

Seed of spirituality

Spirit   **Personality**   **Mental Body**   **Emotional Body**   **Physical Body**

Now, way back here, this little seed of spirituality in the personality, this little seed back here has to try to get up enough gumption to reach into the mental body and into the emotional body and into the you. So, what is happening here? It doesn't do too bad getting into the mental body, but in the mental body you're going to pick up erroneous lessons from the soul of you.

Now remember, the soul is your complete, perfect memory of everything you have ever experienced, whether it is real and true or whether it is your error thought and is not true at all. The soul does not differentiate; it simply records and keeps for all time for you everything that ever has been or ever shall be for you.

So, into the mental body comes this little personality. Right about now you're about four years old, so you have four years of earth experience. Most of it has to do with your home life. You haven't gotten out into the world yet. So, while you're at home, you're more or less safe. One day you're safe, the next day you're not safe. Depends on what's going on in the family. Mommy and Daddy getting along together? Assuming you have Mommy and Daddy together, your world is pretty good, but Mommy and Daddy have a rip-snorting, knock-down, drag-out fight and your world is not so good. Now you're afraid. Now you don't know what's going to happen to you. "What's going to become of me? Is this my fault? Did I do something bad? I must have done something bad. This has got to be my fault."

So, now you've got a load of guilt. Now, guilt is not far away because you all feel guilty because you think you walked out on God, so it doesn't take a whole lot to wake up the feeling of guilt in you. All you have to do is witness a good fight among your parents and you've got a load of guilt that comes right to the surface in that little personality and says to it, "You see that. You were *bad*. You see that. This is *your* fault."

Now, what have you got? You've got a feeling, "I'm not lovable. I am not loved. I am bad. There is something terribly wrong with me; therefore, I will never be loved." Most children by the age of four have established a pretty good idea of whether or not they are going to be loved the rest of their lives or they will never be loved.

Now, that little personality is developing. It's beginning to form ideas and perceptions of its own. Up to this point, it more or less *thought* what it was supposed to think according to the dictates of its environment.

You have to remember, beloveds, you live in two environments. You live in two environments. The one environment is an *internal* environment that you have totally, absolutely created for yourselves. It consists of your ideas of yourself, your opinions of yourself, how you *feel* about you. It consists of your belief system, and I am not referring only to religious beliefs; I'm talking about your belief system upon which you base the way you live. That's your *internal* environment.

Now, your external environment consists of your home, your job, your world around you, your circle of friends, and so forth and how you interact with them. Have you not noticed that you are a very different person when you are alone than you are when you are with people? I don't care who the people are. That you are very different when you are out with people? But when you are home all by yourself with just you and the cat or something, you're a very different person, aren't you?

Now, which environment do you think has the most effect upon the developing personality, the internal or the external? The internal. That is why some people can have a beauteous home, a very fine marriage, a nice job, lots of money, and all of that and still be very unhappy. Because their *internal* environment is not healthy.

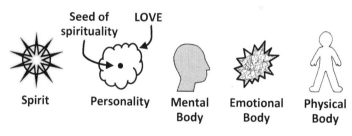

So we have to *activate* love. We have to get love right in the beginning. We have to get love in here. We have to get love into this personality, and that is not as hard to do as one might think because why? It's right next to the Spirit, and what is the Spirit? The Spirit is love.

So, how do you bring that love into the personality so it will constructively affect the mental body and absolutely soothe the chaotic emotional body so that your physical life isn't a sorrowful, poor is me, but is a happy, joyous, haha, haha?

It is simple. Recognizing that you are love. "Oh, you've told us that before. We don't know how to do it. Obviously it's not working. I love myself pretty much excepting when I do something stupid." Oh, we know all that you think.

If a friend did something stupid, would you stop loving them? No. Then why do you stop loving yourselves when you do something stupid. Don't you know that stupidity is part of a human being's earth life? Everybody does something... [To Tinkerbell[1]] I know you don't, but you're not a person. Everybody does something stupid once in a while. Even if you do several something stupids, should you beat yourselves up and stop loving yourself? No, absolutely not.

So, the love that you are is your natural nature. That is your natural environment. That should be the internal environment in which you dwell. And it has nothing, absolutely nothing, to do with your external environment. Absolutely nothing.

When you are in tune with your internal environment, *you are in love.* Not with some person out there, but you live lovingly. You find joy in life. You don't feel downtrodden or beleaguered.

"But you don't know my life. I lost my job, my car was stolen, my cat got run over, my boyfriend ran off with

---

[1] Tinkerbell (also called Tinker) is Gabriel's joyful angelic helper, who has more familiarity with the earth plane than he does.

the fellow upstairs. (Laughter) So, what does one do in a case like that? First of all, you bless the cat to light. You forgive the boyfriend and the fellow upstairs. You release and let go. Why? Because you can't change anything. You can't bring the cat back to life or change the relationship that's going on, and none of what has happened to you is anything that you can change. So what...that's your external environment.

Now, what *can* you change? Your *internal* environment. You change your attitude. Do you say, "Oh well, I'll get another cat, and I am glad he's gone anyway"? No. You recognize that all of that that's happened is the *ego's idea* of what *your* life is, and that's all it is, is the ego's idea of what your life is.

Now, your *real* life, the true life of you, comes from where? Does it not come from back here in the Spirit of you? This little, tiny babe that you've placed in your personality that is the spiritual truth of you? *This* is perfect love, and you've got it in you. It was placed there the moment you were breathed into creation.

So, that has the ability of tracing all the way through into this world, the physical world in which you dwell. But it only has one path that it can go, and that path is through the mental body.

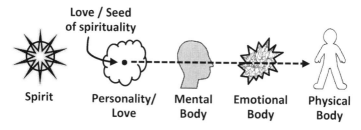

Now, what would love be expressed...how would love be expressed in the mental body? Now remember, the mental body has absolutely no emotion, so you can't say the mental body *feels* happy. The mental body doesn't feel anything. But the mental body, with all of its power, tremendous power, how would the mental body express love?

There's one word: peace. Your mind is at peace.

Now, positive thoughts...positive thoughts have to be *lived*; they just cannot be thought. They have to be an *experience* that you *live*, and in order for that to happen, your mind has to not be engaged in a tangle of worry. When you are worried, your mind is not at peace. When you are afraid, your mind is not at peace. Any form of negativity in your mind is the gift of the ego, because the ego would always want you to be off balance, and how better to keep you off balance than to fling in a worry thought.

It's like you're going along and your mind is at peace and everything, and the ego comes along and flings in a worry thought. "Oh, what was that sound in my auto? Is my car alright, I wonder? I wonder if I should have it checked over? Perhaps I shall tomorrow have it checked over. I thought I heard a weird noise." Or you're walking along enjoying the loveliness of the out of doors and you're thinking, "Thank you, God, for beauty, for beautiful sky. Oh, did I shut the stove off before I left? Oh, I can't remember if I shut the stove off. Perhaps I'd better go back and take another look. Oh, it must be alright. No, I can't remember if I shut it off. If the tea kettle boils down...oh, I'd better go back."

Now, what has happened to your peace of mind? One little, teensy, little worry thought flung in there and the whole time of peace has been blown away.

So, it requires watchfulness, mindfulness. When the ego presents its little game of "I don't think you shut the stove off. Did you hear that noise in your automobile? Oh, you're in for trouble, I know," you have to do one thing: You take yourself up and you say, "I am a child of God and I am dwelling in perfect peace."

Now, this requires watchfulness because the ego is *so* subtle and tricky, so subtle. Have you not noticed how it will lead you down the path of negative thinking before you even realize it? You go into a merchandise place and you decide you're going to buy some clothing. You're feeling very good. It's been a nice day. You got a bonus in the mail and you have money to spend on your garment and you're feeling very...so you go and you select the garments and you try them on and you think, "I must have gained ten pounds. This doesn't look good on me at all. I'm not going to buy this. I've probably gained weight. I must have gained weight. Oh, what's the use. I diet and diet. It's no use. I'm just going to be overweight. That's all there is to it. This is terrible. I don't feel like shopping. I think I'll just go home...or eat." (Laughter)

But do you see how subtly the ego works? Instead of saying, "Well, this garment is not becoming on me at all but I shall select another." And never mind the ten pounds whether it's there or not. You have to be on guard.

Now, let's go back to love for a moment. The ego works the same way with love. It allows you the false security of being in love, and then it starts its little game. "Did you notice that he didn't call when he said he would?"

"Well, he probably got busy...or he's seeing another woman."

"Nah, he wouldn't do that."

"Well, you never know. Men are funny that way." (Laughter)

"I don't think he would. I'll bet you if you called him, he would have some lame-brain excuse."

"I'll prove you wrong. I shall call."

You call. He says, "Oh, I fell asleep in front of the TV and I didn't wake up until eleven o'clock."

"I told you it was a lame-brain thing, didn't I?" (Laughter)

Now, first thing you know, you've got this doubt in your mind. Now you're not sure whether this person you love is really...maybe they're not who you think they are. So what is the ego doing? It's keeping you out of balance. Instead of there being joy in your relationship, now there's doubt, there's mistrust.

Now, all of this goes right back to the mental body and the emotional body. What sets your emotional body on edge *more* than feeling you're losing something? You're losing a loved one, you're losing your job, you're losing your grip on life, you're losing your ability to think clearly. How much fear is wound up in the idea of *losing something*? Your children are moving away, perhaps. Or your son is marrying a girl that you just *know is no good*. Or perhaps the most subtle one of all is when the ego says, "You know, when you get old, you're going to be all alone."

"No, I won't. I'll have my family."

"No, you won't." (Laughter) "Do you realize your grandchildren will be all grown up and off doing their own thing? Your sons and daughters are going to be busy with their own lives. Do you realize when you get old people don't want you around?"

"You know, you're right. They probably don't. What'll I do?"

"Throw in the towel. It's no use." (Laughter)

These are the things that the ego does to you, and you fall in its trap all the time. Because what happens when the ego throws in that little doubt or that little fear? You grab it right up and you *build* on it and the first thing you know, you've got yourself convinced that the only thing you have to look forward to is tragedy of some sort—ill health, poor finances, being all alone, or all three, whatever.

So, what happens here? You have to *know* that you are loved. Now, who's love are you never, ever, ever without? The love of God. And where is that love? Is it in the external environment? No. It's in the internal Self of you. It is that part of you that never dies, that part of you that is forever and ever.

Now, recognizing that and *using* it, consciously using that idea, does many wonderful things for you. Number one, it helps you to recognize how *loved* you are. Once you feel completely loved by God, guess what happens? You are not attached to anything external.

How do you love someone and not be attached to them? Purely, totally, absolutely without fear. You can be so in love with someone that you don't know what end you're on, and if you are unattached to them, you have no fear that they will go out of your life, you have no fear that they will betray you or hurt you. You are in love—truly *in* love—whether there is an object of affection out there or whether there is not, you are in the even, ever-moving, ever-expanding, ever-glorious, and joyous flow of love.

And that means that you love yourself, doesn't it? Then when you do something stupid, what do you do?

You laugh. "Boy, was that dumb. I tell you, kid, you're a pip." (Laughter) There's no condemnation. There's no feeling of "Why did I ever think that? I was so stupid." There's none of that. You live in joy.

Non-attachment is a very powerful thing. Does that mean that you don't give a hoot? Not at all. Some of the people who are the most loving and caring are the ones who have absolutely no attachments. What does it mean to have no attachments? Does that mean that you don't want a lovely house, you don't want a nice auto, you don't want someone wonderful in your life? No, it doesn't.

Non-attachment means that you have such perfect trust in the gift of God, which is perfect love, that it never occurs to you that anything but your highest good is ever going to happen to you. You *trust, completely trust*, and when you completely trust, the windows of heaven open and blessings pour forth because you are in tune with the *one* love that is pure, the one love that is the basis for all other loves: the love of God.

The love of God does not abide by the rules of the ego. The love of God loves you all the time, without exception, no matter what you *think* you have done that would be deserving of not being loved. God doesn't see you at all the way you see yourselves, and is *that* ever a blessing. (Laughter)

The love of God pours itself out on everyone equally the same. The love of God does not see one person greater or lesser than the other. The love of God does not say, "This person is a favorite; that person I can do without." The love of God is equal at all times. It is ever in *perfect balance*. It never is out of balance, like the ego would have you believe that you are. It is in *perfect balance* all the time.

Now, being unattached to the outcome of situations is one of the most difficult things for human beings to realize because you all have the idea of how you want a certain thing to be. What you are not realizing is that by being unattached to the outcome, you are allowing the flow of love/life to take you exactly to the perfect place for you.

Now, *your* idea of the perfect place may not be God's idea, but I'll tell you what...his ideas are a whole lot better than yours. (Laughter) And if you can trust enough to hold to that, then the non-attachment becomes your greatest gift, because no matter what is going on in your external environment, your *internal* environment is completely at peace. Now, instead of having an emotional body that is all awry and panic stricken and everything like that, you have an emotional body that is filled with the flowing of life, of love, of joy. Your mind is at peace, your emotional body is in love, and you are healthy and happy and going forward with all of the truth and ideas that you came into this earth to carry forth.

How many of you think you came into life trusting, and then life happened to you and it was awful? None of you? Good. But so many people in your world think that that's how it is. They really believe that life is terrible, and what they believe is what happens to them. And that's what happens to all of you. It's what you believe. It's your *internal* environment that sets the pace of what happens to you.

During your second war, in the concentration camps, after the war when the allied forces went through the concentration camps, amongst all of the awfulness, they found pictures that were drawn, sometimes just scratched on the wall, of butterflies, of birds, of flowers.

They came across one saying, "I cannot tell if the sun is shining today; there are no windows in here. I cannot see God, but I know that God is present here even though I don't see him, just like I know the sun is present even though I don't see it."

There is in the Spirit of you, in the Spirit of all people, that innate *knowing* that you are love, that truth will out, and that all the awful things that seem to be in the world are the illusion of the maniacal egos of humankind. They have no substance, they come and they go, and life goes on in beauty and in truth. And that is all because you are love—true, pure love—that has nothing to do with the emotions whatsoever but rather has to do with the universal force that can move anything. The greatest power there is, is love, and you're *it*. Absolutely, you are *it*.

Do you have anything to ask of me concerning this day's lesson?

Participant: Good evening, Gabriel. Why is the ego so nasty? (Laughter) It doesn't have any dominion...

Gabriel: Because, beloved entity, its only life, the only life it has is when you believe in it, so in order to keep you entrapped, it has to keep you constantly off balance, because once you gain your God Self, the consciousness of your God Self, then you have no further use of the ego. So it tries constantly to preserve its life and in order to do that, it has to keep you *out* of your God Self.

Participant: I don't understand where God gets its idea that it had to preserve itself or...

Gabriel: Well, actually, human beings created the ego. Now remember, when you *thought* you left God, when you thought you were no longer connected, it left you feeling very vulnerable. And don't forget way back then you lived in a very dangerous...well, no, actually, not any more dangerous than it is today in your time but certainly much less sophisticated. So, you created the ego as a kind of safety device. The ego's job was to keep you *safe*, to let you know if a saber-toothed tiger was creeping up upon you or something of that sort. Well, after a bit, you became...you relied on the ego more and more and more until instead of it becoming your servant, it became your master because it constantly fed you with fear so that you had to depend upon it what *you* believed to be for your safety.

Participant: So, like everything else, we created it.

Gabriel: Absolutely, you did. And it has no power excepting what you give it.

Participant: Do animals have egos?

Gabriel: Oh, they have a *form* of ego, but it is not like the human. It is not as sophisticated, and it truly is their servant. It truly helps them to know when danger is about. And that's all that the ego was ever supposed to do.

Participant: So, are they living in their God Self?

Gabriel: Oh, much more so. Now, don't misunderstand. When an animal lives in its God Self, it relies completely on its higher self. Its instincts, what you call its instincts, is really the God Self of them.

Participant: Good evening, Gabriel. You made the statement that we need to activate love when we're very young in the personality. My question is, is that a factor of our *external* environment or is it something that we come in with?

Gabriel: Oh, indeed, you do.

Participant: The ability to activate it for ourself?

Gabriel: Yes. Children instinctively love. They love. It is only when they are taught *not* to love that they stop loving.

Participant: In our society, we see children that grow up in horrible home atmospheres, and they're wonderful people. And then we see children that have wonderful home life, maybe, and they're not loving and they don't feel loved, apparently. So, I didn't know if it was something as a parent that as parents we should really attempt to give children all the love we possibly could—and I suppose good parents do that anyway...

Gabriel: Why is it that those who have every advantage turn out to be poorly and those who have no advantage turn out to be good? It depends upon what the soul has fed into that personality, and also it depends on what the personality has chosen for its lesson. Sometimes a person learns more through adversity than they do through pleasure, if that is the way they *think*.

Now, there are those who think, "Well, if I suffer enough, I shall be holy," type of thing. Or, what is it you say, "No pain, no gain," type of thing. But when you come to recognize the God Self within you, you don't think in those terms, so you would not create for yourself a life upon the earth of hardship because you know there is no advantage in it.

Participant: So, we do come in with that agenda to either express love or withhold love from our self?

Gabriel: Oh, yes, indeed. If you have a lot of soul memory that tells you you're a terrible person, you're not going to come in feeling good about yourself and therefore feeling that you deserve love.

Participant: And we set that up while we're still in spirit?

Gabriel: Yes, because in spirit you see all of the things that you have *not* seen correctly, so you think, "Well, I'll come back and I shall see this correctly this time." What you're missing is the realization that the past is over, and if you keep looking at the past, you're going to make the future just like it. What you need to do is to recognize the present moment in which you are the child of God—dearly, deeply loved, eternally loved—and base your belief system on *that* rather than on "Well, in this lifetime I was a horrible person, so in this lifetime here I had better suffer for my sins." It's all in the attitude that you have about yourself. But when you are willing to reach into that little portion of spirituality, which is in the personality, and find it and *build* upon it, then is when you find your life filled with joy.

Participant: Can we only do that in a physical body?

Gabriel: No, you can do it anywhere, anytime, wherever you are, whether you are in spirit...

Participant: I guess what I don't understand is, when we're in spirit, why don't we already know that and quit coming back and making mistakes?

Gabriel: We'd love to know! (Laughter) We'd love to know. It's just that you take such an attitude...you get down in that low astral and you will not look up at the light. You stay down there and you believe everything you see there, everything you experience there, never stopping to think that it's all illusion. There's none of it true. And instead of looking up to the light and going *into* the light of understanding and of truth and love, you hang about there and then you decide to reincarnate and you come from that low astral perspective and you create for yourself terrible experiences.

Participant: Okay. I guess I had always assumed that once when we were in spirit, we were truly back in touch with our God Self.

Gabriel: When you let yourself be, you are, but so many people *will not allow it*. They will not allow themselves to come up out of the astral.

Participant: Because they're focused in the wrong direction.

Gabriel: They're focused in the wrong direction.

Participant: Thank you.

Gabriel: Any others? No questions this night? Indeed, it is a miracle, eh? (Laughter) No one has anything to ask? It was so clear? I'm very glad. Yes, Tinker says I do good work. (Laughter) Well, if you have no questions, I guess we shall allow Beloved Woman[2] to come back and claim her body.

Participant: I have a question. (Laughter)

Gabriel: There we go. All I have to do is say, "I'm out of here," and they all get up.

Participant: We don't want you to leave. Beloved Gabriel, you didn't mention the word "vibration" tonight, and I know that when we bring more love into our being, it increases our rate of vibration.

Gabriel: Oh, absolutely it does. Yes.

Participant: And with my personal experience, when I have experienced deep, spiritual love, it seemed like the vibration was really too great for me to actually even incorporate into my other bodies, my emotional and physical bodies.

Gabriel: No, it isn't because it would come in softly and very gently, and it would come in so you must always encourage it. Always encourage it. Don't ever feel, "Oh, I'd better not because..." because that's the ego not letting you have that completeness.

Participant: And as that love comes in, does that affect your chakras and...

Gabriel: It affects the totality of your being. Everything, everything is affected.

Participant: It purifies everything.

Gabriel: It purifies everything. It brings you into the purity in which you were created.

Participant: And it also...you said it restores peace to your mind.

Gabriel: Peace...absolutely it does. It brings you peace. It gets to where no matter what's going on around about you, you are at peace. No matter how chaotic your external environment might be, there is an internal peacefulness that does not ever leave you.

Participant: And if a person is carrying fear—we all have fear blocks, it seems, to this love—as love comes in, as we learn to allow love to come in, does that love just have the effect of reducing the fear and dissolving the fear?

Gabriel: It drives the fear out. Fear and love cannot dwell in the same dwelling. They cannot come and they do not live together, for one will drive out the other. If your fear is great enough, it will drive out love. When you allow the pure love, the true love, to come in, it dissolves the fear. The fear just *has* to go; it cannot abide where love is. Know how it tells you in your Scriptures, "Perfect love casteth out fear," and that is a grand truth.

Participant: It's really the *best* way to move fear out of our beings, isn't it?

Gabriel: Is to love, indeed. That's why the Master taught you, "Love your enemies." You're not afraid of someone you love. And once the fear is gone, the enemy is gone as well. The enemy becomes a friend.

Participant: Thank you.

Gabriel: You are very welcome.

Participant: First of all, it is a pleasure to meet you.

Gabriel: Pleasure to meet *you*.

Participant: I am a teacher of little children, many of whom are filled at the age of six with anger and resentment and hatred. I try to bring love to them. How can I help *them* to find this love too?

Gabriel: Just love them. They will sense it in you and they will want to *be* in that love, and it will rub off on them and they will become more loving.

Participant: I find it very frustrating sometimes. I have my own problems in dealing with it, with *their* anger and resentment and I feel...

Gabriel: Just love them anyway. Love them past it. Just keep loving them.

Participant: Good evening. You've probably given lectures and lectures on the ego. I'm still not quite clear about what exactly it is, and recently I have been introduced to the concept of the "cosmic ego." And what you described tonight was that the ego is basically dropped away, and this idea of the cosmic ego that I just

learned about and don't really understand thus far is that the ego is transformed. You don't really dispense with it.
Gabriel: Oh, it is transformed. Yes, it is. In the transformation of it...when you created the ego, you created it as a safety device to keep you from falling off a cliff or whatever. But as I said early on, you gave it too much power. You began to rely on the ego rather than on the God Self of you.

Now, in its true perspective, as the ego is transformed, then it becomes your *servant*, but until it becomes your servant as it was intended to be, you must not listen to the voice of the ego because the voice of the ego always is toward fear, fear, fear. When the ego is transformed and takes its rightful place, then the fear that it feels it at this point must project is changed rather to perception and to a kind of a broader sense of not always seeing everything in the negative, and it balances itself out.

Participant: So it really is a part of...how would it fit in this diagram that you have?

Gabriel: How would it fit in the diagram? It would become part of the personality. It attaches itself right about in the personality because...your Spirit has no ego. The only thing that has an ego is the personality that you create to come into the earth life.

Participant: So, you could describe it as a tool.

Gabriel: It's a tool. That is what it is meant to be is a tool, but people have allowed it to become their master. They *fear*, and as long as you fear, that means you're listening to the voice of the ego and not the voice of the God.

Participant: You talked to us a lot about the soul being a recording device, and so when we come in, we come in with these memories of our past lives and even our fantasies that we take for being real. In order to let love in...you once gave us an exercise to open up the heart chakra where we just repeated "I am love." Is that a good way to...

Gabriel: The chakras are best left alone. The chakras will automatically come to what they are supposed to be. As long as you're working on being love and being the will of God and so forth, the chakras take care of themselves. To let love in, you have to make room for it, so you have to get rid of your fear and your anxieties and your worry and all of the things that you collect around yourself—your false idols, as it were—and when you get rid of them, then love, God love, comes in.

Participant: So, in order to get rid of them, would reminding yourself constantly when the fear comes about, "I am love. I am a child of God," even if it doesn't feel...

Gabriel: Indeed. You still keep saying it, beloved woman, because *internally* you *know* it is true.

Participant: Sometimes it feels real strong but other times—and I'm sure everyone's had this experience—you're frustrated with yourself or you...

Gabriel: But that is what I dealt with this night. You have to...when those things come, then you know you are in your ego, and at that point is when you have to affirm [strongly] **"I *am* a child of God,"** not [meekly] "I am a child of God." (Laughter) The child of God of you is powerful. It is very powerful and it is so pure and so filled with love that when you *claim* it, when you say, "I *am* a child of God," that immediately sets into motion all of the aspects of your beingness that will remove the fear, remove the anxiety, remove all of the things that you are disparaging about.

Participant: If we...I'm going to say, "blow it," because I'm sure all of us here sometimes have just really gotten annoyed and afterwards you think, "Oh, I'm not really being loving." Or very angry. I'm sure that everyone experiences that real frustration or real anger, and then you stop and say, "Well, I'm not being really loving here. I am not being loving." Is that at a point at which you stop and...

Gabriel: You just say, "Alright, *that* which I just expressed was not loving, but I am a child of God. I forgive myself. I send love to me and to whomever you are angry with or whatever you're angry with, and you just know all is well in my world, for everything is in divine order." And then don't go back and think, "You know, I really should have said this to her. The next time she says that, I know what I am going to do." You don't go there. You stay out of that place.

Participant: I'm a little confused about exactly what happens when you die. If somebody dies...

Gabriel: When they die, they leave the body. You are eternal, so the eternal part of you leaves your body behind. The body is the only thing that dies. And in the spirit world, there are many, many levels; you can go into the light, as we call it, or you can go to the astral plane that is full of illusion, make believe, pretend, and all of that sort of thing.

Participant: Are you in your body to go down to the astral? Do you think that you have a body?

Gabriel: Oh, you think you look just as you did in your physical form.

Participant: Oh. So, let us say if somebody dies, let's say in a tragic accident. What's the best kind of prayer to say for them?

Gabriel: To just ask the angels to take them into the light. Just say to them, "Go into the light. Be bathed in the light," because that takes them out of the astral and they don't get caught down there.

Participant: Because I was thinking that if somebody died that was famous and you have all of these people mourning, that would tend to...

Gabriel: It keeps them right down in the astral. If you want to find Elvis when you pass over, go to the astral plane. He's still down there. (Laughter) And he isn't singing "You saw me crying in the chapel" either. (Laughter)

Participant: Hi Gabriel. I'm relatively new to you and I really appreciate being here tonight. I'm trying to process what you've said from my perspective. As I understand it, the human being has a conscious mind and a subconscious mind, and our subconscious mind is that part of us that is feeding our heart and digesting our food and breathing for us and doing it all perfectly, at least pretty much perfectly. And it's also that part of us that is connected to Spirit, to God, and it's our conscious mind, as you said—well, you didn't say this, but I'm interpreting it—as that part of us that is kind of our watchdog, but it's a small part of us and...is that what our ego is, our conscious mind?

Gabriel: Ego dwells in the conscious mind mostly because that's where it can attack you the best. It can really get you there because...you're subconscious has what you will call an instinctual self-preservation that the conscious mind doesn't have, so the conscious mind depends upon the ego to feed it information. But if you were to bypass the ego and go into the superconscious mind, there you would have a direct line with your Spirit Self and you wouldn't listen to the lies that are in the conscious mind or in the subconscious mind, either one, because you have a lot—I don't mean you only—but everyone has a lot of stuff in the subconscious that isn't true. It's all your concepts of what happened *to* you that are there.

Participant: So, then how do we stay connected to the Spirit and the love instead of our ego? What is fueling the ego, the power and the control? How do we quell that and aspire to Spirit?

Gabriel: By doing what I said this night, keeping yourself aware of the fact you are a child of God and you are eternally loved and that all this stuff around you isn't real. It's all the illusion, and you have to learn to go past the illusion into the truth. When you are happy, you are in truth; when you are not happy, you are in the illusion. It's very easy to tell, very easy to tell.

I'm going to close down now and let Beloved Woman have her body back. She hasn't felt well today and we don't want to overstay ourselves, so I shall have a prayer with you before I leave.

Prayer

*Divine life
that manifests in these, Thy children,
as pure love,
we call You forth and ask that they recognize
Your presence within them,
that they feel the love that is eternal
that never leaves them.*

*Cause them, Great Father,
to be ever, ever aware
that all that they are is in You
and You are in them.*

*The heaven they seek
is a present condition within them.
Help them to see heaven.*

*The love that they search for is a present love.
Help them to know that.*

*Cause them, Father God,
to open the doors of their hearts and minds
into the light of truth that dwells ever with them.
May they be aware of that light
forever and ever.*

And so it is.

About the Author

Reverend Penny Donovan, a natural medium since childhood, was ordained in 1960 at the John Carlson Memorial Institute in Buffalo, NY. She obtained her Doctor of Divinity degree from the Fellowships of the Spirit in Buffalo, NY. In 1964 Rev. Penny founded the Trinity Temple of the Holy Spirit Church in Albany, NY, and served as the pastor there for thirty years. In 1994 she retired from that position to devote full time to spreading the teachings of Archangel Gabriel whom she had channeled from 1987 to 1999. Since Gabriel's departure, Rev. Penny has continued to channel, teach, and conduct spiritual healing sessions in classes and retreats through Sacred Garden Fellowship.

About Sacred Garden Fellowship

Sacred Garden Fellowship (SGF) offers workshops, retreats, and publications that teach practical spiritual tools to help people successfully transform life's challenges. Indeed, the first point in its mission is to "encourage all to become aware of and live from their God Self." SGF, founded in 2009 by Rev. Penny Donovan and Donald Gilbert, is a nondenominational 501(c)(3) nonprofit organization located in the Capitol region of New York. For more information about the organization and its offerings, see www.sacredgardenfellowship.org.

41942702R00024

Made in the USA
Middletown, DE
12 April 2019